The Joy of Schubert

Edited and arranged by Stephen Duro.

T0040783

Yorktown Music Press / Music Sales Limited
London / New York / Paris / Sydney / Copenhagen / Madrid

Exclusive Distributors:
Music Sales Limited
8/9 Frith Street, London W1V 5TZ, England.
Music Sales Pty Limited
120 Rothschild Avenue, Rosebery, NSW 2018, Australia.
Music Sales Corporation
257 Park Avenue South, New York, NY 10010, United States of America.

Order No. YK21868
ISBN 0-7119-6786-5
This book © Copyright 1998 by Yorktown Music Press/Music Sales Limited.

Cover illustration by Brian Grimwood.
Compiled by Peter Evans.
Music edited and arranged by Stephen Duro.
Music processed by Allegro Reproductions.

Music Sales' complete catalogue describes thousands of titles and
is available in full colour sections by subject, direct from Music Sales Limited.
Please state your areas of interest and send a cheque/postal order for £1.50 for postage to:
Music Sales Limited, Newmarket Road, Bury St. Edmunds, Suffolk IP33 3YB.

Visit the Internet Music Shop at http://www.musicsales.co.uk

Your Guarantee of Quality:
As publishers, we strive to produce every book to the highest commercial standards.
The music has been freshly engraved and the book has been carefully designed to minimise
awkward page turns and to make playing from it a real pleasure.
Particular care has been given to specifying acid-free, neutral-sized paper made from
pulps which have not been elemental chlorine bleached.
This pulp is from farmed sustainable forests and was produced with special regard for the environment.
Throughout, the printing and binding have been planned to ensure a sturdy,
attractive publication which should give years of enjoyment.
If your copy fails to meet our high standards, please inform us and we will gladly replace it.

Printed in the United Kingdom by
Caligraving Limited, Thetford, Norfolk.

Allegretto in C Minor
D.915

Composed by Franz Schubert

Allegretto

D.C. al Fine

An Mein Clavier

Composed by Franz Schubert

An Die Musik Op.88, No.4

Composed by Franz Schubert

Andante from Sonata in A Minor D.845

Composed by Franz Schubert

Andante poco mosso

Andante from Sonata in A
Op.120

Composed by Franz Schubert

15

Andante in C
D.29

Composed by Franz Schubert

Andante

Ave Maria Op.52, No.6

Composed by Franz Schubert

Ballet Music from Rosamunde
Op.26

Composed by Franz Schubert

Allegretto moderato

Country Dance from Set No.2

Composed by Franz Schubert

28

Entr'acte from Rosamunde
Op.26

Composed by Franz Schubert

Impromptu In A♭

Composed by Franz Schubert

Allegretto

Ländler from Twelve German Dances

Composed by Franz Schubert

36

Menuett In A
D.334

Composed by Franz Schubert

Allegretto

Trio

Fine

38

D.C. al Fine

39

Marche Militaire Op.51, No.1

Composed by Franz Schubert

Allegro vivace

41

42

43

Minuet D.41, No.20

Composed by Franz Schubert

D.C. al Fine

Moment Musical Op.94, D.780, No.3

Composed by Franz Schubert

Allegretto moderato

47

Scherzo D.593, No.1

Composed by Franz Schubert

50

Serenade

Composed by Franz Schubert

Theme from the Unfinished Symphony

Composed by Franz Schubert

Allegro moderato

Valse from 34 Valse Sentimentales
D.779, No.12

Composed by Franz Schubert

Who Is Sylvia?

Composed by Franz Schubert

Wandering

Composed by Franz Schubert